Maths Together

There's a lot more to maths than numbers and sums;
it's an important language which helps us describe, explore and
explain the world we live in. So the earlier children develop
an appreciation and understanding of maths, the better.

We use maths all the time – when we shop or travel from one
place to another, for example. Even when we fill the kettle we are
estimating and judging quantities. Many games and puzzles
involve maths. So too do stories and poems, often
in an imaginative and interesting way.

Maths Together is a collection of high-quality picture
books designed to introduce children, simply and enjoyably, to basic
mathematical ideas – from counting and measuring to pattern and
probability. By listening to the stories and rhymes, talking about
them and asking questions, children will gain the confidence
to try out the mathematical ideas for themselves – an
important step in their numeracy development.

You don't have to be a mathematician to help your child
learn maths. Just as by reading aloud you play a vital role in
their literacy development, so by sharing the *Maths Together* books
with your child, you will play an important part in developing their
understanding of mathematics. To help you, each book has detailed
notes at the back, explaining the mathematical ideas that it
introduces, with suggestions for further related activities.

With *Maths Together*, you can count on doing the
very best for your child.

To Caroline D.

Acknowledgements

The editor and publisher gratefully acknowledge permission to reproduce
the following copyright material:

Moira Andrew: "Ten Red Geraniums" © Moira Andrew; first published in *One in a Million*,
edited by Moira Andrew (Viking 1992); reprinted by permission of the author. Dave Calder: "Adding It Up"
© Dave Calder 1990; reproduced by permission of the author. John Coldwell: "Socks" © John Coldwell;
from *The Bee's Knees* (Stride 1990); reprinted by permission of the author. John Cotton: "Nature's Numbers"
© John Cotton; reprinted by permission of the author. Gina Douthwaite: "Muddy Mongrel" © Gina Douthwaite;
from *One in a Million*, edited by Moira Andrew (Viking 1992). Edna Eglinton: "Family Visit" © Edna Eglinton
1992; first published in *One in a Million*, edited by Moira Andrew (Viking 1992); reprinted by permission of
the author. Pam Gidney: "Because of Number One" © Pam Gidney; first published in *One in a Million*,
edited by Moira Andrew (Viking 1992); reprinted by permission of the author. Trevor Harvey: "Favouritism"
© Trevor Harvey 1989; from *Poetry for Projects* (Scholastic 1989); reprinted by permission of the author.
Sue Heap: "On the Beach I Saw" and "Tom's Pocket" © Sue Heap 1999. Wes Magee: "What Is a Million?"
© Wes Magee; from *The Witch's Brew and Other Poems* by Wes Magee (CUP 1989); reprinted by permission
of the author. Ian Souter: "Numberless!" © Ian Souter; reprinted by permission of the author.
Charles Thomson: "How Many Peas…" © Charles Thomson; reprinted by permission of the author.

While every effort has been made to obtain permission, there may still be cases in which we have failed
to trace a copyright holder, and we would like to apologize for any apparent negligence.

First published 1999 by Walker Books Ltd
87 Vauxhall Walk, London SE11 5HJ

2 4 6 8 10 9 7 5 3 1

Collection © 1999 Walker Books
Illustrations © 1999 Sue Heap
Introductory and concluding notes
© 1999 Jeannie Billington and Grace Cook

This book has been typeset in ITC Flora.

Printed in Singapore

British Library Cataloguing in Publication Data
A catalogue record for this book is
available from the British Library.

ISBN 0-7445-6838-2 (hb)
ISBN 0-7445-6801-3 (pb)

What's In A Number?

A Collection of Poems

Illustrated by Sue Heap

WALKER BOOKS
AND SUBSIDIARIES
LONDON • BOSTON • SYDNEY

Numberless!

If all the numbers in the world were
rubbed out,
removed,
taken away:
I wouldn't know how old I was,
I wouldn't know the time of day,
I wouldn't know which bus to catch,
I wouldn't know the number of goals I had scored,
I wouldn't know how many scoops of ice-cream I had,
I wouldn't know my phone number,
I wouldn't know the page on my reading book,
I wouldn't know how tall I was,
I wouldn't know how much I weighed,
I wouldn't know how many sides there are in a hexagon,
I wouldn't know how many days in the month,
I wouldn't be able to work my calculator.
And I wouldn't be able to play hide-and-seek!
But I would know
as far as my mum was concerned,
I was still her NUMBER ONE!

Ian Souter

I'm number ONE!

Tom's Pocket

In Tom's pocket he had ...
1 keyring
2 keys
3 tickets
4 pieces of bubblegum
5 badges
6 marbles
7 pencils
8 sweets
9 coins
10 stick-on stars.

How many things did Tom have?

How Many Peas...

How many peas
fit in a thimble?
How many acorns
fit in a matchbox?
How many ping-pong balls
fit in your shoe?
How many baked beans
fit in you?

Charles Thomson

Nature's Numbers

One old observant owl
Two tame tickled trout
Three thirsty throated thrushes
Four fine fantailed fish
Five fantastically famous frogs
Six swiftly swimming salmon
Seven sweetly singing songbirds
Eight engagingly eager eels
Nine nippy neighbourly newts
Ten tenderly tiptoeing tortoises.

John Cotton

Socks

On Monday we wear quiet socks,
Not flash, bang start a riot socks,
Not, Hey you come and try it socks.
On Monday we wear quiet socks.

On Tuesday we wear plain socks,
Not crazy and insane socks,
Not frazzle up your brain socks.
On Tuesday we wear plain socks.

On Wednesday we wear boring socks,
Not pass to me goal-scoring socks,
Not modern abstract drawing socks.
On Wednesday we wear boring socks.

On Thursday. Ordinary socks,
Not horror, shock and scary socks,
Not beastly monsters hairy socks.
On Thursday. Ordinary socks.

On Friday, it's polite socks,
Not glowing in the night socks,
Not give your aunt a fright socks.
On Friday it's polite socks.

At weekends we wear loud socks,
That stand out in the crowd socks
And make our feet feel proud socks.
At weekends we wear loud socks.

John Coldwell

Favouritism

When we caught measles
It wasn't fair –
My brother collected
Twice his share.

He counted my spots:
"One hundred and twenty!"
Which sounded to me
As if I had plenty.

Then I counted his –
And what do you think?
He'd two hundred and thirty-eight,
Small, round and pink!

I felt I'd been cheated
So "Count mine again!"
I told him, and scowled
So he dared not complain.

"One hundred and twenty" –
The same as before…
In our house, he's youngest
And he always gets more!

Trevor Harvey

Muddy Mongrel

One paw
two paws
three paws
four
thousand
paw marks
on the
floor.

Gina Douthwaite

What Is a Million?

The blades of grass growing
on your back lawn.
The people you've met
since the day you were born.

The age of a fossil
you found by the sea.
The years it would take you
to reach Octran Three.

The water drops needed
to fill the fish pool.
The words you have read
since you started school.

Wes Magee

Because of Number One

I'll tell you something funny –
The strangest thing under the sun.
There's never an end to numbers,
Because of Number One.

You think you're clever when you count to twenty –
But then there's twenty-one.
So on you go, and thirty comes –
And then comes thirty-one!

You reach a hundred! Then you think
That all your counting's done.
But no! A little voice inside
Says, "Now a hundred-and-one."

You reach a thousand! Number One
Insists on going on.
You're all worn out. A million comes:
But there's still "A million-and-one."

The person who caused all this trouble
(When I could be out having fun)
Is the man who lived in the dim distant past
And invented Number One!

Pam Gidney

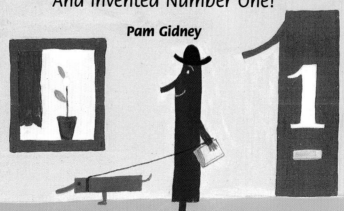

On the beach I saw

1 boat

1 feather

1 piece of driftwood

4 shells

3 pebbles

2 starfish

How many things did I see?

Adding It Up

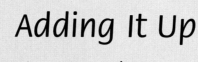

One tomato and one tomato
make two tomatoes.
Two bananas and two bananas
make four bananas.
Four jellies and four jellies
make eight jellies.

Eight feet and eight feet
make sixteen feet.

Sixteen feet in heavy boots
stamping on
eight jellies, four bananas and two tomatoes
make ...

a horrid mess.

Dave Calder

Ten Red Geraniums

Ten red geraniums
sprouting when it's fine,
a slug came slithering
and then there were nine.

Nine red geraniums
glowing when it's late,
a bat came blundering
and then there were eight.

Eight red geraniums
shining bright as heaven,
a magpie moth came munching
and then there were seven.

Seven red geraniums
propped up by sticks,
a wire-worm came wriggling
and then there were six.

Six red geraniums
fiery and alive,
a weevil came wandering
and then there were five.

Five red geraniums
dancing by the door,
a beetle came biting
and then there were four.

Four red geraniums
as vivid as can be,
a caterpillar came crawling
and then there were three.

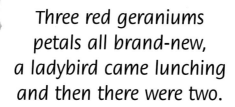

Three red geraniums
petals all brand-new,
a ladybird came lunching
and then there were two.

Two red geraniums
blazing in the sun,
a great-aunt came admiring
and then there was one.

One red geranium –
the only one I've got,
I'll keep it on my window-sill
in its own well-watered pot.

Moira Andrew

Family Visit

Two on a motor bike,
Four in a car,
Six people go to visit
Granny and Grandpa.

Eight people chattering,
In comes Uncle Jim
With cousins Luke and Kylie
And their little brother Tim.

One For Me and One For You

One for me and one for you
If there's one left over then what'll we do?
Take up a knife and cut it in two
So there's one for me and one for you.

Clyde Watson

There are so many of us
We can hardly shut the door:
Granny's only got ten chairs
So two sit on the floor.

I help Granny cut the cake,
Twelve slices for our tea.
Baby Tim won't eat and so
There's an extra piece for me.

Edna Eglinton

About this book

What's In A Number? is a collection of poems which invites children to look at numbers in lots of different ways. You may want to read them through more than once, particularly the ones your child really likes.

"Tom's Pocket" and "Nature's Numbers" both involve counting in small numbers, up to ten and twelve. This may reinforce what children already know and helps them feel more confident. "Muddy Mongrel", "How Many Peas…", "Favouritism" and "What Is a Million?" are about much larger numbers. Children are fascinated by large numbers and the idea of counting on and on. They probably won't be able to understand them yet, but just talking about them and encouraging your child to become familiar with their names is what is important at this stage.

"Numberless!" and "Because of Number One" provide wonderful opportunities for you to talk about how important our number system is. Without numbers we wouldn't be able to answer questions like how many?, how long?, how much? or how old? With just the symbols 0 to 9 we can represent any number we like, no matter how large or small.

In "Socks" and "Family Visit" the counting is in twos. This is the beginning of counting more efficiently, and leads to learning multiplication by two and then by other numbers. "Family Visit", "Adding It Up", "On the Beach I Saw", "Ten Red Geraniums" and "One For Me and One For You" all give children the chance to join in with adding up, subtracting and dividing.

Notes for parents

There are lots of things to count in *What's In A Number?* Reading "Nature's Numbers", your child can match the animals in the pictures with the words. You can also talk about what could come next.

What comes after ten tortoises?

Eleven … enormous elephants!

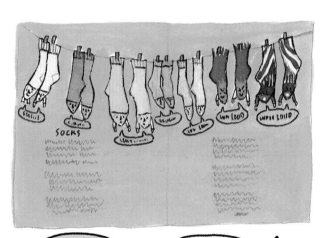

After reading "Socks" together, you can talk about counting in twos, and also about what else comes in pairs – shoes, gloves, eyes and ears, for example.

Let's count how many socks in seven pairs.

2…4…6…8…10…12…14!

How many things are on the beach?

There are plenty of opportunities in the book for children to try adding things up using the pictures as well as the words. You could ask them "How many people visited Granny and Grandpa?" or, much harder, "How many measles spots are there?"

One boat, one feather, four shells – that's six…

As well as looking at all the numbers in the book, try a "number hunt" at home. Look on the phone, video or microwave, on food packets and on the calendar. You can point out that numbers help us answer questions like how long?, how far?, what time? and what date?

Our number's twenty-seven!

And what about Annie house?

27

I wonder how many biscuits there are?

More than twenty. I know that!

Wherever you are, there are things to count – at home, out shopping, on journeys or in the park. Encourage your child to estimate first and then count.

Everyday situations provide opportunities for other number activities as well as counting. Together you can explore different ways of multiplying, comparing, taking away and sharing.

Six for me, three each for you.

You always get more than me.

One go that's left

You can play a game together based on "Tom's Pocket". Collect fifteen small objects in groups (for example, 1 marble, 2 stamps, 3 crayons, 4 sweets, 5 coins) and mix them up. Then cover them while you take one (or two) away. Encourage your child to find a way of working out what's missing.

Children can make a "Book of Special Numbers": their favourite number, their age, Granny's phone number, the year they were born... Encourage them to write and draw the numbers in as many ways as possible, cut them out of magazines, or trace them from books.

Maths Together

The *Maths Together* programme is divided into two sets – yellow (age 3+) and green (age 5+). There are six books in each set, helping children learn maths through story, rhyme, games and puzzles.

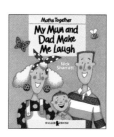

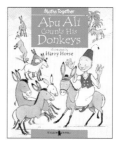